Lizards

Julie Murray

Abdo
Kids

I LIKE ANIMALS!

abdopublishing.com

Published by Abdo Kids, a division of ABDO, PO Box 398166, Minneapolis, Minnesota 55439.
Copyright © 2017 by Abdo Consulting Group, Inc. International copyrights reserved in all countries.
No part of this book may be reproduced in any form without written permission from the publisher.

Printed in the United States of America, North Mankato, Minnesota.

052016

092016

 THIS BOOK CONTAINS
RECYCLED MATERIALS

Photo Credits: iStock, Shutterstock

Production Contributors: Teddy Borth, Jennie Forsberg, Grace Hansen

Design Contributors: Candice Keimig, Dorothy Toth

Cataloging-in-Publication Data

Names: Murray, Julie, author.

Title: Lizards / by Julie Murray.

Description: Minneapolis, MN : Abdo Kids, [2017] | Series: I like animals! |
    Includes bibliographical references and index.

Identifiers: LCCN 2015959205 | ISBN 9781680805321 (lib. bdg.) |
    ISBN 9781680805888 (ebook) | ISBN 9781680806441 (Read-to-me ebook)

Subjects: LCSH: Lizards--Juvenile literature.

Classification: DDC 597.95--dc23

LC record available at http://lccn.loc.gov/2015959205

Table of Contents

Lizards

Tim holds a lizard.

It has scales on its skin.

Lizards have long tails.

Some can lose their tails.

But they grow back!

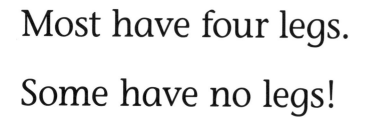

Most have four legs.

Some have no legs!

8

A gecko has **toe pads**.

These help it climb.

10

Lizards live in trees. They live on the ground, too.

They eat bugs.

The iguana eats a leaf.

15

Lizards can be any color.

Some have spots or stripes.

A blue-tailed skink is

easy to spot.

19

Do you like lizards?

Some Kinds of Lizards

beaded lizard

green anole

crested gecko

panther chameleon

Glossary

scales
flat plates that form the outer covering of reptiles.

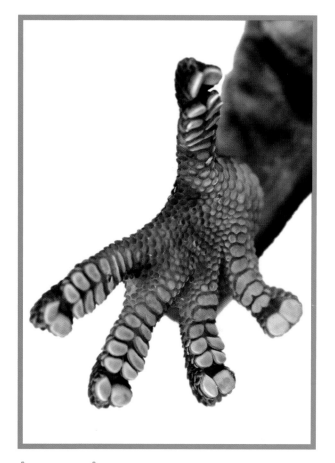

toe pads
special pads on the feet that allow some lizards to climb up surfaces and even climb upside down!

Index

abdokids.com

Use this code to log on to abdokids.com and access crafts, games, videos, and more!

Abdo Kids Code:
ILK5321